the FUN-duh-mental HOUSEHOLD

5

STEPS FOR ORGANIZING YOUR HOME
Using an SOP (Standard Operating Procedure)

Rita McCoy

The Fun-duh-mental Household: 5 Fundamental Steps for Organizing Your Home Using an SOP

Published by Sound Off Publishing
Kissimmee, FL

ISBN: 978-0-9993068-1-9
House & Home Organizing

QUANTITY PURCHASES: Schools, companies, clubs, and other organizations may qualify for special terms when ordering quantities of this title. For information, email soundoffpublishing@gmail.com.

CONTENTS

ACKNOWLEDGMENTS

I would like to acknowledge and thank the people who contributed to this book. Thanks to my husband Anthony McCoy, who co-authored, designed, and provided his perspectives on organizing a thorough household system. I appreciate my copyeditor and sister, Tamara Smith Roldan, who ensured we delivered accurate and quality content, and proofreader Tarah Gibbs Threadgill, who ensured grammar, sentence mechanics, and formatting was consistent. A special thanks to Victoria Wolf of Wolf Design and Marketing, who created a dynamic user-friendly interior design for the book. And, Polly Letofsky, who provided guidance, resources, and an incredible professional team to help complete the project.

I am most grateful to each of you. Thank you so much.

INTRODUCTION

THE FUN-DUH-MENTAL HOUSEHOLD SOP

"Not right now," his soft voice said. These are the famous words of one of my brothers. Those words meant no matter what project he was working on, he would get to it later – much later – or not at all.

Matter of fact, his entire home had been in disarray for years and it wasn't because he didn't have time for it. He was a grand procrastinator and delayed practically everything with his favorite saying, "Not right now."

Fast forward to his lengthy hospital stay. He needed a family member to manage his household while he focused on his medical issues. Unfortunately, not a soul was interested in rummaging through piles of scattered papers, disheveled files in make-shift cabinets, and bills stacked high on top of every table; however, overwhelming love took over and the family did what families do – persevered. It took many hours and several days to locate important documents and determine which bills to pay. The task was a true nightmare with eyes wide open.

If my brother had applied the methods in "The Fun-duh-mental Household SOP" prior to his situation, the family's nightmare would have been a pleasant dream. Imagine: important papers organized in one place or being able to pick up a binder and manage his household effortlessly. By applying the steps in the Household SOP binder, bills would be paid on time with no worries of late fees, penalties, or cancellations along with the family having confidence in managing his household.

Question: What steps would you take to organize a disorganized home, including your own? How would you locate and identify critical documents?

Thankfully, my husband Anthony designed a simple system to smoothly operate and manage our household. With his accounting, auditing, and business skills, he created easy-to-use forms to keep track of household routines. He is an ultimate organizer, and I am the ultimate beneficiary of his organizational skills. Over many years, we have tried, tested, and proven the effectiveness of the *5 Steps in The Fun-duh-mental Household*, and hopefully you will become an ultimate beneficiary as well.

The Fun-duh-mental Household outlines 5 fundamental methods to organize your important contacts, logins, projects, finances, and documents.

Based on this tested system, *The Fun-duh-mental Household* was originally thought to be designed for people living solo. But it turns out married couples like me and people in other relationships can benefit from organizing their homes using an SOP (Standard Operating Procedure).

The main objective is to run your household like a well-organized business by using an effective and efficient system. In other words, get rid of any clutter.

If you live solo, NOW is the time to get organized and organize for the future. If you live with someone, NOW is the time to plan ahead. If anything happens to you, who will pay your bills or know where important papers are located?

Is your house in order?

Are there times when you forget when a particular bill is due? Or maybe you can't remember who performed maintenance work on your home.

I assume you know where your house and car keys are, but what about the deed to your property? Do you have important people in your life? If so, where is that list located? Who should be called in case of emergencies? What day of the month do you pay your rent or mortgage, auto insurance, or utility bill?

 The Fun-duh-mental Household is a system designed to help you put your house in order and to prepare you for both predictable and unpredictable circumstances in life. As the saying goes "life happens" or "change is inevitable." By being prepared for the expected and unexpected, it will relieve stress and anxiety for you, your spouse, family, and friends should you ever need their assistance in running your household.

Are you ready to get organized?

Whether you live alone, live with a trusted friend, significant other or spouse, this easy-to-follow SOP will help you organize the important aspects of your household. As a matter of fact, an organized household works wonders on your mental health; you simply find things quicker.

Of course, each household is different; however, there are some commonalities: emergency contacts, computer logins, finances, property deeds. Add to that, birth certificates, marriage licenses, etc. Also, within your household, you probably have daily, weekly, monthly, or annual tasks you perform to maintain your home. We'll show you a quick and easy method to stay on top of these tasks using some handy forms.

Wouldn't it be great if you had a household handbook you could customize for your residence?

We designed *The Fun-duh-mental Household* book to include a variety of forms to help you maintain an efficient household. As with businesses that use a Standard Operating Procedures (SOP) manual to help employees manage the day-to-day work operations, a Household SOP can help you manage all routines pertaining to your home. This Household SOP is two-fold: (1) it is designed for you to stay organized with routine tasks, and (2) it will help not only you, but any family member or friend maintain normal operations of the household when you are not available.

What are the benefits?

The Household SOP is a great reference. It is designed to manage and organize your residence. You customize the forms to reflect your home. The methods described in this book are straightforward and easy to complete.

What do finances have to do with an organized household?

Knowing your sources of income is paramount. For some, they concentrate on the employment paychecks per month, but for others, income could be from 401K, social security, pension, investments, or business accounts. The bill pay, income statement, cash flow, and net worth forms in this handbook will assist you in keeping track of all your finances.

Why is a Household SOP important?

Here is something to think about. What if you live alone and something happens to you? Perhaps you have an extensive stay in a hospital for a medical procedure. Do you have important information scattered throughout your household? If so, now is the time to gather all pertinent information into one place. That one place is where the Household SOP comes in handy. It is up to you to provide access to the Household SOP to whomever your trusted confidant is, which could be a family member, a best friend, your attorney, or an advocate; they could easily refer to the SOP and keep your home running smoothly when you are away.

Another example would be, let's say you are married, and your spouse handles every aspect of the household from paying the bills to filing tax returns. Or maybe your spouse knows exactly the time of year for auto maintenance or the annual cleaning of the furnace. If they leave for three months, do you know what bills to pay and when? Or do you have to search through a mountain of paper to determine what to pay? All of this can be stressful. So, let's eliminate the not knowing, the paper mountain, and the stress.

The Fun-duh-mental Household SOP puts everything in one place so you are not confused or frustrated. The ability to go to the binder and find what you need right away will prove helpful and timesaving.

Where do you keep your important documents?

Do you own property? Do you have a deed to your property? Do you know where you placed your important papers? Are they hidden so that you and nobody else can find them?

The "VIP (Very Important Papers)" section of this handbook provides you the opportunity to start identifying the whereabouts of your documents. Again, this eliminates guesswork for you and assists family and friends who may eventually be responsible for knowing the location of these legal papers or certificates.

Since each household is unique, you can customize the forms provided to fit your needs. Analyze the forms that work best for your residence, and in each section, we'll give instructions on how to use them.

WHAT IS COVERED?

In ***The Fun-duh-mental Household***, you will find the following sections:

1. **Contacts & Logins** — Important people to call and logins to remember.

2. **Projects** — Routine tasks and products

3. **Finance** — Bill pays, cash flow, income statement, and net worth

4. **VIP** — Very Important Papers (and their whereabouts)

5. **Helpful Tips** — Additional tips on organizing each section

We'll take you through the steps. Let's get started.

WHAT YOU'LL NEED

What you will need to get started:

1. A 3-ring binder, 5 Tabs, and a 3-hole punch.

    Tabs (Also See Table of Contents Form in the Appendix Section):

    ❏ **Contacts & Logins**

    ❏ **Projects**

    ❏ **Finance**

    ❏ **VIP (Very Important Papers)**

    ❏ **Helpful Tips/Notes**

2. A storage bin, large folder, or file drawer for very important papers.

3. A few hours to devote to this project.

4. A good attitude as you start to gather all the necessary components that will make up your personalized Household SOP binder.

The exhibits in each section are your examples. There are blank forms for you to copy, use, and customize in the Appendix section.

- Exhibit A: Points of Contact

- Exhibit B: Login

- Exhibit C: Routine Tasks

- Exhibit D: Products to Order

- Exhibit E: Bill Pay

- Exhibit F: Cash Flow

- Exhibit G: Income Statement

- Exhibit H: Net Worth

- Exhibit I: VIP (Very Important Papers) Whereabouts

Use the following "To Do List" to organize your thoughts on what you'll need to complete behind each tab.

TO DO LIST

Step 1 — Contacts & Logins

- ☐ ....
- ☐ ....
- ☐ ....
- ☐ ....
- ☐ ....
- ☐ ....
- ☐ ....
- ☐ ....
- ☐ ....
- ☐ ....
- ☐ ....
- ☐ ....

Step 3 — Finance

- ☐ ....
- ☐ ....
- ☐ ....
- ☐ ....
- ☐ ....
- ☐ ....
- ☐ ....
- ☐ ....
- ☐ ....
- ☐ ....
- ☐ ....
- ☐ ....

Step 2 — Projects

- ☐ ....
- ☐ ....
- ☐ ....
- ☐ ....
- ☐ ....
- ☐ ....
- ☐ ....
- ☐ ....
- ☐ ....
- ☐ ....
- ☐ ....
- ☐ ....

Step 4 — VIPs

- ☐ ....
- ☐ ....
- ☐ ....
- ☐ ....
- ☐ ....
- ☐ ....
- ☐ ....
- ☐ ....
- ☐ ....
- ☐ ....
- ☐ ....
- ☐ ....

Step 5 — Review Helpful Tips section when creating your Household Standard Operating Procedure Binder.

NOTES

....

....

....

....

....

....

....

....

....

....

....

....

....

....

....

....

....

....

....

....

STEP 1 — CONTACTS & LOGINS

CONTACTS & LOGINS

Points of Contact Form (Exhibit A) is where you create a list of individuals (family, friends, service vendors, etc.) to call in case of an emergency. If you live alone, this form will prove valuable for your close relatives or friends recruited to assist you. For those readers who are married, your contacts may be different from your spouse so both of you should create separate lists. After you complete the Points of Contact Form, place it behind the Contacts Tab within the binder.

If you have a password protected electronic version of your contacts, let a family member or best friend know how to access your phone or computer where your contacts are stored.

The Points of Contact Form should not take long to create. Chances are you already have a contact list in your phone, computer, or email. Print it out and place it in the binder. A couple of factors to consider: only include important individuals rather than every person you've ever met and remember to update this list yearly as connections and networks may change.

EXHIBIT A

POINTS OF CONTACT		
FAMILY	**Location—Description**	**Phone Number**
Example: Name	*City, State*	*xxx-123-4567*
John Doe	Chat, TN	xxx-123-4567
Moe Doe	Chat, TN	xxx-234-5678
FRIENDS – ASSOCIATES	**Location—Description**	**Phone Number**
Michael	Town, MO	xxx-345-6789
Mary	Town, MO	xxx-456-7890
SERVICES – VENDORS	**Location—Description**	**Phone Number**
Accountant - Joe	Town, MO	xxx-678-9012
Doctor - SoSo	Town, MO	xxx-789-0123

Login Form (Exhibit B)

Do you have hundreds of logins and passwords? Which accounts are most important that affect the household?

In this section with the Login Form, you will be able to quickly locate your logins and passwords for accounts linked to commodities such as travel, medical, shopping and food, along with Wi-Fi networks, computers, phone, or emails accounts.

Give special attention to membership accounts or other subscriptions that may automatically charge your credit cards. Make a note as to the month each credit card will be charged. Some accounts may require cancellation by a specific date. Make note of that in the comments section.

With regards to passwords, if you use codes for your passwords, that's fine. Just make sure your family and/or trusted friend knows how to decode.

After you have completed your Login Form, place it in your binder under Contacts & Logins.

EXHIBIT B

LOG-IN	
TRAVEL	**User ID | Password | Comments**
Airlines Name	email - Ab345 2500 award points
MEDICAL	
Hospital Name	email - Bb456 - Med Records
INVESTMENT – FINANCIAL	
Bank Name	email - Cc567 - Credit Card
HOUSEHOLD	
Store Name	email - Dd678 - Discounts
GENERAL ACCOUNTS	
COMPUTER NAME	
OTHER	

NOTES

STEP 2 —
PROJECTS

PROJECTS

Routine Tasks (Exhibit C)

Let's move on to what you need to accomplish daily, weekly, monthly, and annually to operate your household.

When listing routine tasks on the Routine Tasks Form, it should reflect what you do on a regular basis. For example, under Daily, you may have some procedures you perform daily, such as, taking apple cider vinegar each morning or doing an exercise routine each evening. Customize the form to fit you. Give it some thought.

What routine tasks are suitable for running your household? What must you do weekly, monthly, quarterly, semi-annually, or annually? Review the example provided to conceptualize categories for your household.

This form helps eliminate confusion; it also serves as a checklist of what you need to accomplish and what has been completed. We all have certain routines in our lives. Here you have the opportunity to organize your projects.

EXHIBIT C

TITLE	ROUTINE TASKS	Daily	J	F	M	A	M	J	J	A	S	O	N
	Daily												
Health	Exercise mind and body; eat healthy	x											
Health	Take Multi-vitamins	x											
Security	Secure doors/alarm	x											
	Monthly												
Finance	Pay bills via Bill Pay/Checks		x	x	x	x	x	x	x	x	x	x	x
Health	Detox body		x	x	x	x	x	x	x	x	x	x	x
Household	Purchase household items online		x	x	x	x	x	x	x	x	x	x	x
Automobile	Check fluid levels: oil, brakes, power steering, window wash, tires		x	x	x	x	x	x	x	x	x	x	x
Indoor	Check/clean vent on dryer		x	x	x	x	x	x	x	x	x	x	x
	Quarterly												
Indoor	Check and change air filters				x			x			x		
Outdoor	Cut plants and bushes				x			x			x		
	Semi-Annual												
Automobile	Scheduled Maintenance							x					
Finance	View/print investment statements							x					
Indoor	Check, clean HVAC filter system under lower rack							x					
Indoor	Maintenance/tune up HVAC unit (Apr Oct)							x					
Medical	Dental exams							x					
	Annual												
Automobile	Insurance cards, renew registration; if needed—renew driver license (Jan–Feb)		x										
Finance	Order free credit reports: Experian, TransUnion, Equifax		x										
Finance	Prepare tax returns		x										

MONTH

Products to Order (Exhibit D)

How many products do you have under your bathroom counters, in your kitchen pantry, or out in your garage? If your home is like most households, you have an array of products, many of which could be ordered monthly online.

The Products to Order form is designed as a monthly ordering and inventory tracking document for products often purchased online for your home. By ordering online, it reduces the number of trips to the store for products. Budget wise, you are dispensing funds once a month instead of several times throughout the month.

Write down the type of item and mark the month in which you need to order the product. You can place a quantity under the month or a checkmark. For efficiency, our tip is to order products once a month and use this form as an inventory and tracking tool. By ordering once a month, you'll save time and money.

EXHIBIT D

PRODUCTS TO ORDER

Instruction: 1st - Under month write-in number (#) of items to o
2nd - On bottom of page, in the long boxes below, enter cost
order # and delivery date.

Type	Item	Jan	Feb	Mar	Apr	May	Jun	Jul	Aug	Sep	Oct	Nov
Example: Appliance	Furnace filter 18x20x1	3										
	HOUSEHOLD											
Air fresh												
Air fresh												
Appliance												
Appliance												
Auto	Floor mats	2										
Auto												
Batteries	AA batteries			1								
Batteries												
Body	Bath Soap				2		2		2		2	
Body												
Bulbs												
Bulbs				3					3			
Deodorant			2		2		2		2		2	
Dishes												
Disinfect				2			2			2		
Eye	Dry Eye Drops		1		1		1		1			1

NOTES

....

....

....

....

....

....

....

....

....

....

....

....

....

....

....

....

....

STEP 3 — FINANCE

FINANCE

In this section, you will work on the following forms: Bill Pay, Cash Flow, Income Statement, and Net Worth.

Bill Pay (Exhibit E)

When is your next electric bill due? When do you pay rent or mortgage? How about your auto payment, when and how much? **The Bill Pay Form** helps keep track of each bill you pay. List the description, memo, login (if needed for online billing), due date, and amount.

In the January through December columns, either put a checkmark when you pay the bill, or the amount you paid. This document organizes bills that need to be paid by a certain date. Each month, it is a useful tool for you to stay on top of your payments.

EXHIBIT E

BILL PAY — Year _____

Description	Memo	Login ID, Password	Due	Jan	Feb	Mar	Apr	May	Jun	Jul	Aug	Sep	Oct	No
Company Name	Insurance	login in, password	1st	$25										
Company Name	Utility	login in, password	15th	$70										

NOTES:

Cash Flow Form (Exhibit F)

The power of the spreadsheet! It is the glue that keeps it all together, making an efficient and effective household possible.

What is the foundation that all 5 fundamental steps have in common? The answer: money management. How so?

1. Contacts & Logins: Assist with securing logins/passwords to protect financial contents.

2. Projects: Manage tasks and products to avoid costly remedies.

3. Finance: Oversee valuable possessions/money.

4. VIP: Store important documents for easy access of valuable data and financial safekeeping.

5. Helpful Tips: Additional information to help you save time and money.

Managing cash flow is critical for reaching the goals of each fundamental aspect while accomplishing your desired result: to operate your household like a well-organized business. "Cash Flow" is the name of the game!

The **Cash Flow Form** shows the amount of funds coming in and going out of a specific account. For our illustration, it will be your checking account. A few benefits associated with using this money management tool includes:

- Increasing awareness of how much money you have available at any given time.

- Determining when to pay bills or purchase items to avoid over-spending and enhance savings.

- Allowing money positioning to be viewed weeks or months in advance.

EXHIBIT F

CASH FLOW

One= 1st half; Two=2nd half	JAN ONE	JAN TWO	FEB ONE	FEB TWO	MAR ONE	MAR TWO	APR ONE	APR TWO	MAY ONE	MAY TWO	JUN ONE	JUN TWO	T
Balance - Checking Acct	0	1,150	(23)	977	3,802	4,377	7,202	8,202	11,027	12,027	12,572	13,147	
Adjustment	150	0											
BANK STATEMENT BALANCE	150	1,150	(23)	977	3,802	4,377	7,202	8,202	11,027	12,027	12,572	13,147	
Salary	5,000		5,000		5,000		5,000		5,000		5,000		
Pension		3,000		3,000		3,000		3,000		3,000		3,000	
Other Income		250		250		250		250		250		250	
INCOMING	5,150	4,400	4,977	4,227	8,802	7,627	12,202	11,452	16,027	15,277	17,572	16,397	
Allowance/Pocket Money	300		300		300		300		300		300		
Automobile: gas, loan	100	350	100	350	100	350	100	350	100	350	100	350	
Credit Cards	0	3,998		0						2,280		2,323	
Dues/Fees					75						75		
Emergency													
Groceries/Household	400		400		400		400		400		400		
Insurance	500		500		500		500		500		500		
Medical													
Mortgage/Rent	2,500		2,500		2,500		2,500		2,500		2,500		
Savings													
Services/Repairs					350						350		
Taxes													
Telephone/Cable	50	75	50	75	50	75	50	75	50	75	50	75	
Travel & Entertainment													
Utilities - electric, gas	150		150		150		150		150		150		
Other Expenses													
OUTGOING	4,000	4,423	4,000	425	4,425	425	4,000	425	4,000	2,705	4,425	2,748	
REMAINING	1,150	(23)	977	3,802	4,377	7,202	8,202	11,027	12,027	12,572	13,147	13,649	

Income Statement Form (Exhibit G)

Where does all your money come from? You may have several sources, not just employment. Maybe you have a pension, social security, or investment income as well.

Create the Household Income Statement by listing your income sources from work, pension, social security, interest, dividends, royalties, and gifts. It is refreshing to view your sources at a glance.

Next, list your household expenses including auto loans, credit cards, dues, HOA, insurance, repairs, utilities, taxes, and others.

It's imperative that your home is run like a well-organized business when it comes to finances. We believe having your finances in order and organized gives you peace of mind.

EXHIBIT G

INCOME STATEMENT			
Example: Checking Acct	*Bank Name, address, city, state zip - Phone (800) xxx-xxxx,*	*$1,000*	*nephew / user id, password*
INCOME	**General Information**	**Amount**	**Notes**
Employment	*Company name, address*	5,000	
Pension			
Social Security			
Interest & Dividend		100	
	Total Income	**5,100**	
EXPENSES	**General Information**	**Amount**	**Beneficiary /Notes**
Auto Payment		400	
Credit Card		200	
Credit Card		500	
Charity			
Dues & Fees	Auto Club	100	
Groceries	Food, Household	350	
Health products			
HOA - Homes Owner Assn			
Home - Mortgage/Lease		1,500	
Insurance- Accidental			
Insurance - Auto			
Insurance - Medical			
Insurance - Medicare			
Insurance Vision (optical)			
Services & Repairs			
Taxes		200	
Utilities	Company name, address	150	
Utilities - Phone		70	
Other			
Other			
Total Expenses		**3,470**	
Total Income minus Total Expenses = REMAINING FUNDS		**1,630**	

Note:

Knowledge of spreadsheet formulas are helpful to utilize automatic math calculations. Otherwise, you will need a calculator to complete the forms and a large eraser.

The adjustment column is used to reconcile your checking account balance, which should equal your bank statement.

If you have negatives (outgoing exceeds incoming), the quick remedy is to spend less or shift expenses to another week.

Net Worth Form (Exhibit H)

And finally, wouldn't you like to know what you are worth? With the Net Worth Form, list your accounts like checking, savings, and investments such as CD's, IRA/401K, money markets, stocks and bonds, venture capital, and others. How about your property? List property you own and its value.

Now look at your debts. Do you have an auto loan, credit cards, rent/mortgage, and other debts? List them all.

Math Time:

Add up your bank account balances, investments, and property totals, then SUBTRACT your debt. The remaining is your Net Worth.

EXHIBIT H

NET WORTH				
Example: Checking Acct	Bank Name, address, city, state, zip. Phone (800)xxx-xxxx	$1,000	"sister, nephew, etc"	ID: 1234, Password: Abc123
ACCOUNT	LOCATION	AMOUNT	BENEFICIARY	NOTES
BANKS				
Checking Acct				
Saving Acct				
Holiday Acct				
Other				
Other				
INVESTMENTS				
CDs				
IRA /401k				
Money Market				
Stocks/Bonds				
Venture Capital				

NOTES

....

....

....

....

....

....

....

....

....

....

....

....

....

....

....

....

....

....

....

STEP 4 — VIP (VERY IMPORTANT PAPERS)

VIP (VERY IMPORTANT PAPERS)

Your VIPs (Very Important Papers) (Exhibit I) are classified as your birth certificate, marriage license, deeds, life insurance, wills and testaments, etc. Where do you store your vital documents? And, please, don't say in a shoebox, under the bed, in the attic, or on top of that pile of clothes. The point is, are your VIPs scattered and disorganized throughout your home?

Place your VIPs (Very Important Papers) in a storage bin, folder, file drawer, password-protected electronic file, or fireproof safe. Take the time to complete this extremely important step. It is for you, your close family members, best friend, advocate, or Power of Attorney should you need their services.

For some, you may want to store your VIPs in a fireproof safe or other secure place. That is fine as long as a trusted confidant knows where to find them.

Have you given thought to where to place them if there is ever a fire, flood, or other damage in your home? Make sure wherever you store your VIPs, you can find and retrieve them quickly. By storing them in one place, they're easier to locate versus trying to find them if they are scattered throughout your home.

Electronic Backup: Do you have a digitized version of important papers? VIPs can be backed up electronically. You simply scan all your VIPs into your computer or secure cloud platform. Don't forget to inform whoever is responsible for running your household where and how to access them.

EXHIBIT 1

VIP - WHEREABOUTS

Where Are The Documents Located?

Example: Durable Power of Attorney	Box in back of clothes closet / In the House—Where?	Copy with "name of person" / With a Person—Who?	With lawyer "name, location" / Lawyer's Office— Who/Where?
Documents and Certificates			
Auto Loans, Titles			
Bank Accounts			
Birth, Marriage, Baptism, College Transcripts			
Certificate of Deposit/Stocks/Bonds/Mutual Funds			
Lease			
Mortgage statements, deeds, bill of sale			
Passport			
Employment/Social Security/Retirement Pension			
Insurance			
Insurance including Accidental			
Life, Health, Home, Auto, Personal Property			
Medical bills			
Personal Wishes			
1. Will and Testament, Beneficiary Designations			
2. Medical Power of Attorney for Health Care; health medical affairs			
3. Durable Power of Attorney; business, legal, financial affairs			
4. Lady Bird Deed; avoid probate and pass your property to your loved ones while maintaining eligibility for Medicaid.			
5. Obituary and final arrangements			

PLEASE CONTACT YOUR LAWYER AND SUBSTANTIATE THAT ALL THE ITEMS IN "PERSONAL WISHES" ABOVE, HAVE BEEN COMPLETED, ESPECIALLY: 1. Will ... 2. Medical POA ... 3. Durable POA ... 4. Lady Bird Deed. THESE ITEMS ARE EXTREMELY IMPORTANT TO CIRCUMVENT OR MINIMIZE UNCERTAINTIES SURROUNDING THE INTRODUCTION OF GOVERNMENT INVOLVEMENT IN YOUR FINANCIAL AFFAIRS.

VIP List

Below is a list of documents you should consider storing, organizing, and identifying their whereabouts (if applicable). Some forms may require you to contact a lawyer to prepare, for instance, a Durable Power of Attorney.

Auto Titles	Marriage License
Bank Accounts	Medical bills
Beneficiary Designations	Medical Power of Attorney
Birth Certificate	Mortgage statements, deeds, bill of sale
Deeds	Other: Personal sentimental, or heirloom possessions, safe deposit box, etc.
Durable Power of Attorney	Passport
Health Insurance	Pre-paid funeral arrangements
Insurance policies (home, auto, personal property)	Retirement Pension Benefits
Lady Bird Deed	Social Security Card
Leases	Stock Certificate/Bonds
Life Insurance Policies	Tax files, receipts, records, returns
Loan Certificates	Wills/Trusts/Estate Plans

STEP 5 — HELPFUL TIPS

HELPFUL TIPS

About Paper Clutter

We want you to be able to locate documents quickly without searching under stacks of disorganized paper clutter.

- You do not need to hold on to every single piece of mail received. You may want to toss restaurant or grocery receipts after a month or two.

- Avoid holding on to unnecessary files and documents.

- You may be required to keep some papers for an extended period of time, such as birth certificates, life insurance policies, marriage licenses, pension plans, social security cards, and tax documents.

- Organize all your files in a storage bin, file cabinet, or safe. Always know where they are and how to get to them quickly.

More about Contacts

- When creating your contact list of the most important people in your life, include emergency contacts as well.

- Also, include financial institutions, income/employer, medical, services, and vendors.

- Your Contact list is important in case your designee has to notify others.

More about Bill Pay

- With bill pay, remember to list automatic payments, due dates, and amounts.

- Bills that are transferred automatically on a monthly or quarterly basis should be noted.

More about Beneficiary Designations

- Save time and headaches by listing a beneficiary on your bank and investment accounts. This will help safeguard your property and accounts.

- The beneficiary could be your relatives, friends, or associates. This important step is often overlooked and can cause accounts to be inaccessible until after probate is complete.

More about the VIPs (Very Important Papers)

- When organizing your VIPs, concentrate especially on these documents: wills, power of attorney, bank statements, house deeds, car titles, property insurance, medical insurance, income statements, and investments.

- In the event that you become disabled or pass away, this is when you really need your designated person to know where everything is and to easily locate your VIPs.

- Expose your designee to the whereabouts.

- For digitized VIPs, make sure your designee knows how to access your electronic devices.

NOTES

IN CONCLUSION

If you have completed all of the forms — contacts, logins, routine tasks, products to order, bill pay, cash flow, income statement, net worth, the whereabouts of your important papers, and, finally, the review of some helpful tips – your binder is complete. You now have a binder filled with useful information to operate your home efficiently. Equally so, when you are unable to run your home, a family member, a friend, a confidant, or whomever you choose to help out, can pick up your SOP and continue running your household.

We advise that you revisit this book monthly to make sure you're staying on track with your SOP. Doing so will ensure there is smooth and ongoing order in managing your home.

Continue moving forward. The Appendix of Forms in the next section will aid in maintaining an effective and efficient household.

Congratulations!

NOTES

....

....

....

....

....

....

....

....

....

....

....

....

....

....

....

....

....

....

APPENDIX OF FORMS

1. Table of Contents Form

2. Points of Contact

3. Login

4. Routine Tasks

5. Products to Order

6. Bill Pay

7. Cash Flow

8. Income Statement

9. Net Worth

10. VIP (Very Important Papers) – Whereabouts

TABLE OF CONTENTS	
Contacts & Logins	**Tab 1**
Points of Contact	
Login	
Projects	**Tab 2**
Routine Tasks	
Products To Order	
Finance	**Tab 3**
Bill Pay	
Cash Flow	
Income Statement	
Net Worth	
VIP - Very Important Papers	**Tab 4**
Whereabouts	
Helpful Tips/Notes	**Tab 5**

POINTS OF CONTACT		
FAMILY	Location—Description	Phone Number
FRIENDS – ASSOCIATES		

SERVICES — VENDORS	Location—Description	Phone Number

LOG-IN	
TRAVEL	**User ID | Password | Comments**
MEDICAL	
INVESTMENT – FINANCIAL	
HOUSEHOLD	
GENERAL ACCOUNTS	
COMPUTER NAME	

OTHER	User ID | Password | Comments

OTHER	User ID | Password | Comments

TITLE	ROUTINE TASKS		MONTH											
		Daily	J	F	M	A	M	J	J	A	S	O	N	D
	Daily													
	Monthly													
	Quarterly													
	Semi-Annual													

TITLE	ROUTINE TASKS		MONTH												
	Annual	Daily	J	F	M	A	M	J	J	A	S	O	N	D	
	Travel	Daily	J	F	M	A	M	J	J	A	S	O	N	D	

TITLE	ROUTINE TASKS		MONTH												
	As Needed	Daily	J	F	M	A	M	J	J	A	S	O	N	D

PRODUCTS TO ORDER

Instruction: 1st - Under month write-in number (#) of items to order. 2nd - On bottom of page, in the long boxes below, enter cost $$, order # and delivery date.

Type	Item	Jan	Feb	Mar	Apr	May	Jun	Jul	Aug	Sep	Oct	Nov	Dec

PRODUCTS TO ORDER

Instruction: 1st - Under month write-in number (#) of items to order. 2nd - On bottom of page, in the long boxes below, enter cost $$, order # and delivery date.

Type	Item	Jan	Feb	Mar	Apr	May	Jun	Jul	Aug	Sep	Oct	Nov	Dec

PRODUCTS TO ORDER

Instruction: 1st - Under month write-in number (#) of items to order. 2nd - On bottom of page, in the long boxes below, enter cost $$, order # and delivery date.

Type	Item	Jan	Feb	Mar	Apr	May	Jun	Jul	Aug	Sep	Oct	Nov	Dec

PRODUCTS TO ORDER

Instruction: 1st - Under month write-in number (#) of items to order. 2nd - On bottom of page, in the long boxes below, enter cost $$, order # and delivery date.

Type	Item	Jan	Feb	Mar	Apr	May	Jun	Jul	Aug	Sep	Oct	Nov	Dec

CASH FLOW

One= 1st half; Two=2nd half	JAN ONE	TWO	FEB ONE	TWO	MAR ONE	TWO	APR ONE	TWO	MAY ONE	TWO	JUN ONE	TWO	TOTAL
Balance - Checking Acct													
Adjustment													
BANK STATEMENT BALANCE													
Salary													
Pension													
Other Income													
INCOMING													
Allowance/Pocket Money													
Automobile: gas, loan													
Credit Cards													
Dues/Fees													
Emergency													
Groceries/Household													
Insurance													
Medical													
Mortgage/Rent													
Savings													
Services/Repairs													
Taxes													
Telephone/Cable													
Travel & Entertainment													
Utilities - electric, gas													
Other Expenses													
Other Expenses													
Other Expenses													
OUTGOING													
REMAINING													

CASH FLOW

One= 1st half, Two=2nd half	JUL ONE	JUL TWO	AUG ONE	AUG TWO	SEP ONE	SEP TWO	OCT ONE	OCT TWO	NOV ONE	NOV TWO	DEC ONE	DEC TWO	TOTAL
Balance - Checking Acct													
Adjustment													
BANK STATEMENT BALANCE													
Salary													
Pension													
Other Income													
INCOMING													
Allowance/Pocket Money													
Automobile: gas, loan													
Credit Cards													
Dues/Fees													
Emergency													
Groceries/Household													
Insurance													
Medical													
Mortgage/Rent													
Savings													
Services/Repairs													
Taxes													
Telephone/Cable													
Travel & Entertainment													
Utilities - electric, gas													
Other Expenses													
Other Expenses													
Other Expenses													
OUTGOING													
REMAINING													

INCOME STATEMENT

INCOME	General Information	Amount	Notes
	Total Income		

EXPENSES	General Information	Amount	Beneficiary / Notes

EXPENSES	General Information	Amount	Beneficiary / Notes
Total Expenses			
Total Income minus Total Expenses = REMAINING FUNDS			

NET WORTH				
ACCOUNT	LOCATION	AMOUNT	BENEFICIARY	NOTES
BANKS				
INVESTMENTS				

ACCOUNT	LOCATION	AMOUNT	BENEFICIARY	NOTES
PROPERTY				
DEBIT				
	NET WORTH			

VIP - WHEREABOUTS

Where Are The Documents Located?

	In the House—Where?	With a Person—Who?	Lawyer's Office— Who/Where?
Documents and Certificates			
Personal Wishes			

ABOUT THE AUTHOR

RITA MCCOY, author of ***The Fun-duh-mental Leader***, served as executive director of Sense of Security, a nonprofit organization that serves breast cancer patients who are struggling financially. She was responsible for fundraising, financials, operations, board development, program oversight, and staff management.

Rita McCoy has held positions as executive director, adjunct professor, marketing and communications director, community relations director/executive producer, and television broadcasting public relations professional. She holds a Master of Special Studies in Applied Communications from the University of Denver and a B.A. in Business Administration from Columbia College.

Rita McCoy is an Emmy Award-winning television executive producer. In her role as community relations director/executive producer at KTVD-TV in Colorado, she worked closely with community and nonprofit leaders. She served on numerous committees and boards and served as board president of the Colorado Nonprofit Association and is an Honorary Trustee of the Women's Foundation of Colorado.

Rita enjoys traveling with her husband, playing the piano, volunteering at local charities, attending networking socials, and spending time with her friends and family.